DOING WORK WITH SIMPLE MACHINES

WORKING WITH
SCREWS

RONALD MACHUT

PowerKiDS press.

New York

Published in 2020 by The Rosen Publishing Group, Inc.
29 East 21st Street, New York, NY 10010

Copyright 2011; revised edition 2020

Editor: Elizabeth Krajnik
Book Design: Reann Nye

Photo Credits: Cover Simon Battensby/Getty Images; p. 5 Butterfly Hunter/Shutterstock.com; p. 6 Clear Shot/Shutterstock.com; p. 7 il21/Shutterstock.com; p. 9 Ekaterina Grivet/Shutterstock.com; p. 11 Alliance/Shutterstock.com; p. 12 Nor Gal/Shutterstock.com; p. 13 Morphart Creation/Shutterstock.com; p. 14 Mohd Kafii Isa/ EyeEm/Getty Images; p. 15 Everett Historical/Shutterstock.com; p. 17 Alexander Lobanov/Shutterstock.com; p. 18 KTSDESIGN/Science Photo Library/Getty Images; p. 19 Anna Berdnik/Shutterstock.com; p. 21 Katja Kircher/Maskot/Getty Images; p. 22 Tomsickova Tatyana/Shutterstock.com.

Cataloging-in-Publication Data

Names: Machut, Ronald.
Title: Working with screws / Ronald Machut.
Description: New York : PowerKids Press, 2020. | Series: Doing work with simple machines | Includes glossary and index.
Identifiers: ISBN 9781538345320 (pbk.) | ISBN 9781538343630 (library bound) | ISBN 9781538345337 (6 pack)
Subjects: LCSH: Screws–Juvenile literature.
Classification: LCC TJ1338.M25 2020 | DDC 621.8'82–dc23

Manufactured in the United States of America

CPSIA Compliance Information: Batch #CSPK19. For Further Information contact Rosen Publishing, New York, New York at 1-800-237-9932

CONTENTS

WHAT IS A SCREW?

Screws are all around us. You might not even notice them. Screws hold things together or in place. When you apply force to the top of a simple wood screw by turning it with a drill or screwdriver, the screw twists directly into another **material**, often wood or plaster. Other screws are used to lift things or to put **pressure** on another object.

The screw is one of six simple machines. A simple machine is a **device** with few or no moving parts. These devices are used to modify, or change, motion and force to do work.

MECHANICAL MARVELS

The other simple machines are the inclined plane, the wheel and axle, the pulley, the wedge, and the lever.

WEDGE

SCREW

LEVER

Compound machines are devices that are made up of more than one simple machine. A pair of scissors, which is made up of two levers and two wedges, is held together in the center by a screw.

SCREW PARTS

A screw is a **cylinder**-shaped piece of metal with a winding **ridge**, called a thread, around its length, which is called the shaft. At one end of most types of screws, there is a flat or rounded head with a **slot** into which a screwdriver's tip fits. At the other end of most screws, the cylinder comes to a point.

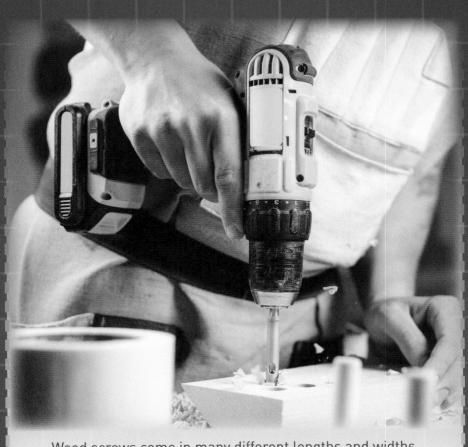

Wood screws come in many different lengths and widths. When using a larger wood screw, you need to drill a hole in the wood to keep the wood from splitting.

There are many different kinds of screws. Cap screws and machine screws hold machine parts together. Screws also take form in everyday objects such as ceiling fans and airplane **propellers**. Even though these objects may not look like screws, they work like a simple wood screw.

SCREWS ARE SPECIAL

← ----------------------------------- →

A screw's thread is actually an inclined plane. As rotational, or turning, force is applied to the top of a wood screw, the plane of the thread meets and lifts the material around it.

All simple machines provide mechanical advantage, which is the machine's ability to multiply the mechanical force applied to the load. The mechanical advantage of a screw depends on how thick the cylinder is. It also depends on how close together the ridges of the threads are. The closer together the threads are, the greater the mechanical advantage of the screw.

Think of this mountain as a screw. It's much easier to get to the peak if you take a path that winds around the mountain rather than walking straight up. The path around the mountain is the thread of the screw.

9

HOW DO SCREWS WORK?

Screwdrivers drive a screw into or pull it out of a material, such as metal or wood. The tip of a drill or screwdriver is placed in the slot at the top of the screw and twists the head of the screw.

Some materials have an **interlocking** thread inside them that the screw's thread should meet. For example, the thread on the inside of a bottle cap is meant to interlock with the thread around the mouth of the bottle. However, if the two threads don't meet the right way, the screw will jam, or stop. The bottle or container won't be completely closed then.

Some of your favorite foods might come in a container with a screw-top lid. Most containers with screw-top lids are airtight to keep foods fresher longer.

THE SCREW PUMP

Archimedes, an ancient Greek **mathematician**, is believed to have invented the screw pump, the first machine that used the idea of the screw, in the third century BC. The screw pump is also called an Archimedes' screw.

People have used Archimedes' screws to empty water out of leaking ships and flooded mines. They have also been used to water crops.

The Archimedes' screw is a machine with a large metal screw sometimes inside a metal pipe. This machine lifts water—or other materials, such as sawdust—from lower ground to higher ground with less effort than lifting buckets. A windmill or handle at an end of the pipe turns the screw. As the screw turns, it lifts water up and out of the top of the pipe.

SCREWS IN HISTORY

Since Archimedes invented the screw pump, people have used screws in a number of ways. For thousands of years, people have used the screw press, which was most likely invented in the first or second century BC in Greece, to press clothing. They're also used in wine and olive-oil presses. Today, screws like this are called power screws.

MECHANICAL MARVELS

Metal screws and nuts didn't appear until the 15th century. These screws are called machine, or machinery, screws.

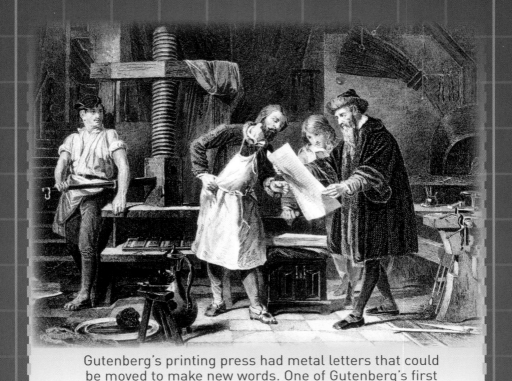

Gutenberg's printing press had metal letters that could be moved to make new words. One of Gutenberg's first projects was a Bible. He printed only 180 copies.

Around 1440, German craftsman Johannes Gutenberg used the idea of the screw press for winemaking to build the first screw press for printing books. In the late 1500s, inventors used Gutenberg's ideas to create a screw press for making coins.

DOING WORK WITH SCREWS

People have been using screws to make their jobs easier for thousands of years. Since the **Industrial Revolution**, people have used screws to do jobs in factories. Some screw presses are used in forging, which is the shaping of metal by applying pressure. Screw presses can bend, cut, stamp, or flatten sheets and pieces of metal.

Other screw presses are used to compact, or press together, materials. Today, many of these machines are powered by engines or computers. However, in the past, they were built on the idea of the simple screw. The factory screw press applies different amounts of pressure as needed.

Many industries use vises, like the one pictured here, to hold materials in place.

EVERYDAY SCREWS

Many people use screws every day. There are screws in many places all around you. Most of the screws you see around your classroom and home are holding things together or in place. The chairs you sit on, the **hinges** on doors, and the lightbulbs in lamps are all held together or in place by a screw.

Another screw you might often see is called a bolt. A bolt is a special kind of screw used to hold things together. It has a flat end and a matching nut, or a ring of metal with interlocking threads.

Drill bits are another type of screw. When attached to a drill, these can make holes in wood and other materials.

STRONG SCREWS

Screws are very strong! People also use screws to help lift heavy loads. Screw jacks, such as the car jack or house jack, are used to lift and hold loads. Screw jacks work by changing rotational motion into linear, or up and down, motion.

A car jack is a machine that allows a person to slowly raise a car in order to make repairs or replace a flat tire. House jacks allow workers to raise a whole house above its foundation, or base. This is often done so workers can rebuild or strengthen the foundation.

When a person turns the screw on a car jack, the jack gets taller and lifts the car.

COMPOUND SCREWS

Screws are often used with other simple machines to create compound machines. An example of a compound machine that uses a screw is the corkscrew. This compound machine has two levers and a screw. When a person turns the handle on top, the screw pushes into the cork and the levers rise. When the person pushes the levers down, the screw pulls the cork out of the bottle.

A bicycle is also a compound machine. It has wheels and axles, levers, and a screw. The seat is adjusted by turning a screw, moving the seat, and fastening the seat in place with the screw.

GLOSSARY

compound: Made up of two or more parts.

cylinder: A solid object shaped liked a tube.

device: A tool used for a certain purpose.

hinge: A metal piece that attaches a door, gate, or cover to something and allows it to open and close.

Industrial Revolution: An era of social and economic changes marked by advances in technology and science.

interlock: To connect or lock together.

material: Something from which something else can be made.

mathematician: A person who is an expert in mathematics.

pressure: A force that pushes on something else.

propeller: Paddle-like parts on a plane or a ship that spin to move the craft forward.

ridge: A raised part or area.

slot: A narrow opening, groove, or passage.

INDEX

WEBSITES

Due to the changing nature of Internet links, PowerKids Press has developed an online list of websites related to the subject of this book. This site is updated regularly. Please use this link to access the list: www.powerkidslinks.com/dwsm/screws